CREATIVE
chi n

ROBYN MARTIN

ISBN 1-74022-373-X

© 2003 Text – Robyn Martin
© 2003 Photographs – Concept Publishing

Published in 2003 by R&R Publications Marketing Pty Ltd
ACN 083 612 579

PO Box 254, Carlton North, Victoria 3054, Australia
Phone +61 3 9381 2199 Fax +61 3 9381 2689
Email: info@randrpublications.com.au
Web: www.randrpublications.com.au

Printed through Bookbuilders, Hong Kong

Cover photo: Chicken with Beans & Walnuts (p. 25)

introduction

Chicken has to be one of the most popular food choices for a meal these days. And that popularity is well-deserved – chicken has proved itself as a versatile, low-fat, great-tasting meat.

Add a simple sauce, a few seasonings or a scrumptious stuffing and you know you will have the basis of a successful meal. Remove the skin for a low-fat option and be wary of using fatty ingredients such as cream or cheese if you are looking after your heart health.

warm CHICKEN SALAD

WITH ORANGE & YOGHURT DRESSING

1 tablespoon chilli oil

350g chicken tenderloins

2 oranges

175g packet mixed small
 salad greens

1 cup torn basil leaves

ORANGE DRESSING

1/2 teaspoon grated orange
 rind

1 cup unsweetened natural
 yoghurt

1/4 cup orange juice

Heat oil in a frying pan. Cook tenderloins for 2 to 3 minutes or until cooked. Peel oranges with a small paring knife, removing all the pith. Cut oranges into segments, cutting either side of membranes. Toss chicken, orange, salad greens and basil together. Pour dressing over and serve immediately.

ORANGE DRESSING

Mix orange rind, yoghurt and orange juice together.

SERVES 4.

SMOKED CHICKEN SALAD

WITH *mango* DRESSING

Use canned mangos to get the mango puree for the dressing.

1 double skinless smoked
   chicken breast
2 spring onions
1/4 cup chopped parsley or
   fresh coriander
6 x 1.5cm slices French bread
1 clove garlic
Small salad greens

MANGO DRESSING
1/2 cup mango puree
2 tablespoons lemon juice
1 teaspoon prepared mustard
Freshly ground black pepper

Cut chicken flesh into strips. Trim spring onions and cut into 1cm slices on the diagonal. Mix chicken, spring onions and parsley or coriander together. Place bread on an oven tray. Crush and peel garlic. Rub garlic over bread. Grill bread until dried and golden on both sides. Wash and dry salad greens. Toss chicken mixture, bread and salad greens together. Serve with Mango Dressing.

MANGO DRESSING

Mix mango puree, lemon juice, mustard and pepper together.

SERVES 3.

CURRIED *peanut* CHICKEN NIBBLES

125g packet salted peanuts

1 teaspoon curry powder

1/2 cup toasted breadcrumbs

2 eggs

2 tablespoons cornflour

18 chicken nibbles

3 tablespoons oil

Place peanuts in a food processor and finely chop. Alternatively finely chop with a knife. Mix peanuts, curry powder and breadcrumbs together. Lightly beat eggs and cornflour together. Dip chicken nibbles in egg mixture then in crumb mixture. Heat oil in a roasting dish. Place chicken nibbles in dish. Turn to coat in oil. Bake at 180°C for 20 minutes or until cooked. Serve warm or cold.

MAKES 18.

SPICY CHICKEN *nibbles*

1 cup dry breadcrumbs

3 tablespoons finely chopped parsley

1 tablespoon finely chopped basil

$1/2$ cup grated parmesan cheese

$1/2$ teaspoon salt

1 teaspoon Tabasco sauce

2 eggs

2 tablespoons oil

$1/2$ bag frozen chicken nibbles

Mix dry breadcrumbs, parsley, basil, parmesan cheese and salt together. Beat Tabasco sauce and eggs together. Dip chicken nibbles into egg mixture then breadcrumb mixture. Place oil in a baking dish. Swirl to coat base. Place chicken in dish and bake at 190°C for 20 minutes or until cooked, turning once during cooking.

SERVES 6 TO 8.

spicy GRILLED CHICKEN WINGS

1kg chicken wings

4 cloves garlic

4 tablespoons finely chopped fresh coriander

3 teaspoons ground coriander

3/4 teaspoon chilli powder

Chopped fresh coriander or parsley

Cut wing tips from chicken wings and use for stock or discard. Crush, peel and finely chop garlic. Mix garlic, fresh and ground coriander and chilli powder together. Rub over chicken and stand for 30 minutes. Cook chicken under a hot grill for 10 minutes. Turn and cook other side until juices run clear when tested. Serve hot or cold, garnished with chopped fresh coriander or parsley.

MAKES ABOUT 14.

CHICKEN & HORSERADISH *filo* PARCELS

Try this for a hot start to an intimate dinner for two.

4 sheets filo pastry
1 cup fresh breadcrumbs
2 tablespoons fresh rosemary leaves
2 single skinless, boneless chicken breasts
1 tablespoon prepared Dijon mustard
2 tablespoons horseradish sauce
Oil spray

Place one sheet of filo on a board. Scatter two tablespoons of breadcrumbs and one teaspoon of rosemary leaves over sheet. Top with a second sheet of filo and continue with breadcrumbs and rosemary leaves. Keep stacking filo, breadcrumbs and rosemary in this manner. Cut pastry stack in half vertically. Spread both sides of chicken with mustard. Place one chicken breast on top of each filo stack. Drizzle horseradish sauce over each chicken breast and wrap up as for a parcel, folding in sides before rolling. Place on a baking tray. Brush or spray with oil. Bake at 220°C for 10 minutes. Turn oven to 180°C and bake for a further 30 minutes. Serve sliced.

SERVES 2.

GRILLED CHICKEN WITH ROASTED CAPSICUM
AND *tomato* SAUCE

4 red capsicums
8 skinless chicken drumsticks
$^1/_4$ cup sundried tomato pesto
1 large tomato

Cut capsicums in half, deseed and place cut side down on a grill rack. Place chicken on grill rack and grill capsicum and chicken until capsicum skin starts to blister. Remove capsicum from grill and continue to cook chicken until juices run clear. It will take about 15 minutes to grill the chicken. Remove skin from capsicum and place capsicum in a blender or processor with pesto. Blend or process until smooth. Cut tomato in half. Remove seeds and core and chop flesh into small cubes. Serve chicken with roasted capsicum and tomato sauce, topped with tomato cubes.

SERVES 4.

tandoori CHICKEN

Tandoori chicken is traditionally cooked in a special oven called a "tandoor". There are many variations of this recipe so adapt the ingredients to what's in your spice cupboard.

6 single boneless, skinless
   chicken breasts
2 tablespoons lemon juice
1 teaspoon salt
3 cloves garlic
1 cup unsweetened natural
   yoghurt
$^1/_4$ teaspoon chilli powder

1 teaspoon ground ginger
2 teaspoons ground
   coriander
2 teaspoons ground cumin
$^1/_2$ teaspoon ground
   cardamom
Freshly ground black pepper
1 teaspoon turmeric

Cut slashes in top of each chicken breast. Sprinkle lemon juice and salt over and set aside while preparing tandoori mix. Crush, peel and finely chop garlic. Mix garlic, yoghurt, chilli, ginger, coriander, cumin, cardamom, pepper and turmeric together. Spread mixture all over chicken. Marinate in refrigerator overnight if possible for the flavours to develop, or compromise if needs be and leave at room temperature for about 1 hour. Barbecue or grill chicken until it looks dry on the outside and flesh is cooked, turning during cooking and basting with marinade.

SERVES 4 TO 6.

grilled CHICKEN TANDOORI

If you haven't got the time for all the spice mixing for your own tandoori mix, try this using a prepared paste.

1/4 cup tandoori paste
1/2 cup unsweetened natural yoghurt
8 skinless chicken drumsticks
1/4 cup chopped salted peanuts
1 tablespoon chopped fresh chives

Mix tandoori paste and yoghurt together. Brush quickly over chicken. Place on a grill rack and grill for 20 to 25 minutes, turning once during cooking. When chicken juices run clear, place on a serving platter. Mix peanuts and chives together. Sprinkle over chicken.

SERVES 4.

indian CHICKEN

500g chicken tenderloins
4 cloves garlic
1 onion
1 cup unsweetened natural yoghurt
2 to 3 tablespoons prepared tandoori paste
1 tablespoon ground coriander
2 teaspoons ground cumin
1 tablespoon grated root ginger
1 tablespoon peanut oil
2 tablespoons tomato paste
1 tablespoon chopped fresh coriander

Cut chicken tenderloins in half lengthwise. Crush, peel and chop garlic. Peel onion and finely chop. Mix yoghurt, tandoori paste, coriander, cumin and root ginger together. Toss chicken in this. Marinate for as long as possible. Heat oil in a large frying pan and saute onion and garlic for about 5 minutes until onion is clear. Add chicken mixture and toss quickly, cooking until chicken is cooked. Stir in tomato paste. Serve with raita (sliced cucumber, salt and chopped mint mixed with yoghurt) and poppadoms. Garnish with fresh coriander.

SERVES 4 TO 6.

YUMMY MANGO *curried* CHICKEN

¹/₂ cup mango chutney

¹/₂ cup unsweetened natural yoghurt

1 tablespoon Madras curry powder

4 boneless, skinless chicken breasts

¹/₄ cup roughly chopped blanched peanuts

1 tablespoon chopped parsley or coriander

Mix chutney, yoghurt and curry powder together. Spread over chicken. Place in a roasting dish. Sprinkle peanuts over top of chicken breasts. Bake at 190°C for 25 to 30 minutes or until chicken juices run clear when tested and peanuts are golden. Serve garnished with chopped fresh parsley or coriander.

SERVES 4.

greek-STYLE STEAMED CHICKEN

4 skinless, boneless chicken breasts
2 tablespoons lemon juice
Freshly ground black pepper
1 clove garlic
1/4 cup pitted olives
2 tablespoons chopped parsley
1/4 cup lemon juice
2 tablespoons olive oil
1 tablespoon capers

Place chicken in an ovenproof dish. Pour first measure of lemon juice over and grind pepper over chicken. Cover and bake at 190°C for 20 minutes or until cooked. Crush and peel garlic. Place garlic, olives, parsley, second measure of lemon juice and oil in the bowl of a food processor or blender. Process or blend until smooth. Slice chicken. Arrange on a plate and serve with olive mixture spooned over. Garnish with capers.

SERVES 4.

CHICKEN, *pumpkin*
& CHICKPEA CURRY

This recipe features regularly on our family meal menu. Use any boneless chicken cut.

700g piece pumpkin
8 boneless, skinless chicken thighs
300g can chickpeas
435g jar korma curry sauce
Fresh coriander leaves

Wrap pumpkin in plastic wrap and microwave on high power for 5 minutes or until almost cooked. Peel and cut into cubes. Cut chicken thighs in half. Drain chickpeas. Place chicken, pumpkin, chickpeas and curry sauce in a saucepan. Wash jar out with about quarter of a cup of hot water and add to saucepan. Cover and cook for about 25 minutes. Serve with steamed rice and garnished with coriander.

SERVES 4 TO 6.

CHICKEN satays

Make your own satays if you prefer to by threading 1.5cm-wide strips of boneless, skinless chicken onto wooden satay sticks.

$1/2$ **cup unsweetened natural yoghurt**
1 tablespoon green curry paste
1 tablespoon tomato relish
12 plain chicken satays
Chapattis or naan bread
Tomato salsa

Mix yoghurt, curry paste and relish together in a shallow dish. Place satays in this, turning to coat. Grill or barbecue satays for 5 to 7 minutes or until chicken is cooked. Warm chapattis wrapped in a paper towel in the microwave for $1\,1/2$ minutes. Serve satays in a chapatti with tomato salsa.

SERVES 4 TO 6.

THAI green CURRIED CHICKEN

Kaffir lime leaves can be bought dried at Asian speciality stores or fresh at some fruit and vegetable shops.

8 boneless, skinless chicken thigh fillets
2 tablespoons Thai green curry paste
425g can coconut cream
2 kaffir lime leaves
2 tablespoons cornflour
3 tablespoons water
1 tablespoon Thai fish sauce
1 lime
Fresh basil leaves

Place chicken in a saucepan with curry paste and cook over a medium heat until curry paste smells fragrant. Add coconut cream and lime leaves. Mix together cornflour and water. Mix into coconut milk mixture. Cover and simmer for 15 to 20 minutes or until chicken is tender. Stir in fish sauce. Cut lime into wedges and mix through curry. Serve garnished with fresh, torn basil leaves.

SERVES 4.

thai-STYLE CHICKEN CURRY

This is something I often put together when I need to prepare a meal with speed. Use the concept for your own variation and never be limited by not having a particular ingredient.

2 onions

3 cloves garlic

1 tablespoon peanut oil

1 tablespoon green curry paste

6 boneless, skinless chicken thighs

400g can coconut cream

1 medium tomato

1/2 cup unsweetened natural yoghurt

2 tablespoons chopped fresh coriander

Peel onions and chop finely. Crush, peel and chop garlic. Heat oil in a medium saucepan and saute onions and garlic for 5 minutes or until onion is clear. Add curry paste and cook for 30 seconds or until paste spices smell fragrant. Cut chicken thighs in half lengthwise. Add to saucepan. Pour in coconut cream. Cover and simmer for 15 to 20 minutes or until chicken is cooked. Cut tomato in half. Remove core and cut flesh into cubes. Add to chicken with yoghurt and coriander. Bring to boiling point but do not boil. Serve with steamed rice.

SERVES 4 TO 6.

spicy INDIAN CHICKEN & POTATOES

Peanut oil is best for this dish, if available.

6 medium potatoes
1 head broccoli
$1/2$ small cauliflower
3 tablespoons oil
1 tablespoon yellow mustard seeds
1 teaspoon curry powder
$1/2$ teaspoon sugar
1 cup chicken stock
500g chicken tenderloins
2 tablespoons chopped fresh coriander or parsley

Peel and dice potatoes. Cut broccoli and cauliflower into florets. Heat oil in a large saucepan. Add mustard seeds and curry powder and cook, stirring, for 30 seconds to 1 minute, or until spices smell fragrant. Add sugar and vegetables. Toss well. Add chicken stock. Bring to the boil and cook for 10 minutes. Add chicken tenderloins and cook for 5 minutes or until chicken is cooked and mixture almost dry. Serve sprinkled with fresh coriander or parsley.

SERVES 4.

chinese CHICKEN, RICE & PEANUTS

2 cups cooked long-grain rice

2 spring onions

1 tablespoon peanut oil

500g chicken tenderloins

8 brown flat mushrooms

2 tablespoons chopped parsley

1/4 cup roasted peanuts

PEANUT DRESSING

1 teaspoon prepared minced ginger

1/4 cup crunchy peanut butter

2 tablespoons soy sauce

1 tablespoon sesame oil

2 tablespoons lemon juice

Cook rice to packet directions. Drain. Trim spring onions and slice finely. Heat oil in a wok or heavy frying pan and stir fry chicken and spring onions for 5 minutes or until chicken is cooked. Slice mushrooms and add to pan. Stir fry for 1 minute. Add rice and toss dressing through. Stir fry until rice is hot. Garnish with chopped parsley and peanuts.

PEANUT DRESSING

Mix ginger, peanut butter, soy sauce, sesame oil and lemon juice together.

SERVES 4.

CHICKEN *balls*

WITH SOY & GARLIC SAUCE

1 spring onion
4 boneless, skinless chicken thighs
1/4 cup soft breadcrumbs
1 teaspoon finely grated root ginger
Pinch chilli powder
1/2 teaspoon salt
1/2 cup soy and garlic sauce

Trim spring onion and chop roughly. Roughly chop chicken. Place spring onion in a food processor with chicken. Process until chicken is finely chopped but not paste-like. Alternatively mince chicken and spring onion. Mix in breadcrumbs, ginger, chilli powder and salt until just combined. Roll tablespoonsful into balls with wet hands. Simmer in boiling water for 3 minutes or until balls rise to the surface and are cooked through. Remove with a slotted spoon and drain well. Serve hot with toothpicks and soy and garlic sauce.

MAKES 22.

FRIED *rice*

Try smoked chicken in this for a change.

4 cups cooked rice	*3 tablespoons peanut oil*
4 rashers bacon	*2 teaspoons grated root ginger*
3 spring onions	*200g can shrimps*
2 eggs	*1 1/2 cups cooked chicken*
1 tablespoon sherry	*1 tablespoon soy sauce*

Spread cooked rice on oven trays and refrigerate uncovered overnight. Alternatively, put trays in a 180°C oven for 15 minutes to allow rice to dry. Turn rice occasionally. Derind bacon and cut into strips. Trim and finely slice spring onions. Lightly beat eggs and sherry together. Cook bacon in a wok or large frying pan until crisp. Remove from wok and crumble. Heat about one tablespoon of the measured oil in wok and cook half the egg mixture to make a small omelet. Remove from wok and repeat with remaining egg. Cut omelets into thin strips. Heat remaining oil in wok. Saute ginger and spring onions for 1 minute. Remove from wok and set aside. Add rice and stir fry for 5 minutes or until lightly browned. Drain shrimps and add bacon, ginger, chicken, omelet strips and soy sauce. Heat mixture thoroughly.

SERVES 4 TO 6.

sweet & sour CHICKEN

1 onion
2 sticks celery
1 carrot
$^1/_2$ green capsicum
432g can pineapple pieces
  in juice
$^1/_4$ cup water
2 teaspoons ground ginger
1 tablespoon golden syrup

2 tablespoons white vinegar
$^1/_2$ teaspoon Tabasco sauce
2 single boneless, skinless
  chicken breasts
2 tablespoons cornflour
3 tablespoons peanut oil
1 teaspoon salt
Snow pea sprouts

Peel onion and cut into eighths. Trim celery and destring. Cut into 1cm slices on the diagonal. Peel carrot and slice finely. Remove core from capsicum and cut flesh into thin slices. Drain pineapple, reserving juice. Mix juice, water, ginger, golden syrup, vinegar and Tabasco sauce together. Cut chicken into 1cm strips. Toss in cornflour. Heat oil in a wok or frying pan and stir fry chicken in batches for 2 to 3 minutes or until cooked. Drain on absorbent paper. Add vegetables and pineapple to wok and stir fry for 3 minutes. Pour in pineapple juice mixture and cook for 2 minutes. Season with salt. Return chicken to wok. Bring to the boil and serve immediately garnished with snow pea sprouts.

SERVES 4.

CHICKEN WITH *beans* & WALNUTS

2 single boneless, skinless
  chicken breasts
2 teaspoons sherry
1 teaspoon soy sauce
1 teaspoon water
$1/4$ teaspoon sugar
1 teaspoon cornflour
Salt

Pepper
1 teaspoon peanut oil
Extra peanut oil
$1/2$ cup walnuts
200g fresh or frozen French
  beans
2 cloves garlic
$1/4$ teaspoon sesame oil

Cut chicken into bite-sized pieces. Place chicken in a bowl with half the sherry, the soy sauce, water, sugar, cornflour, and salt and pepper to taste. Pour the measured peanut oil over and set aside for 30 minutes. Heat 2 to 3cm of peanut oil in a wok or large frying pan. Add walnuts and stir fry for about 2 minutes, taking care they do not burn. Drain and set aside. Drain oil from wok leaving about one tablespoon. Trim beans if necessary. Cut in half crosswise. Crush, peel and mash garlic. Heat oil and stir fry chicken over a high heat until it changes colour. Remove from wok and set aside. Reduce heat. Stir fry beans for 2 minutes. Remove and set aside. Add garlic and saute over a low heat. Increase heat and add chicken, remaining sherry and beans. Stir fry for 5 to 8 minutes or until chicken is cooked. Stir in walnuts and sprinkle sesame oil over top. Serve immediately.

SERVES 2 TO 3.

barbecued

OR BAKED CHINESE CHICKEN

1 medium chicken

3 cloves garlic

2 tablespoons honey

2 tablespoons sherry

2 tablespoons soy sauce

1 tablespoons cornflour

Cut chicken through breast bone and open chicken out. Crush, peel and finely chop garlic. Mix garlic, honey, sherry, soy sauce and cornflour together. Brush over chicken. Place chicken over hot barbecue coals and barbecue for about 45 minutes or until juices run clear, basting with honey mixture regularly during cooking. Alternatively bake at 190°C for 45 minutes or until cooked, also basting during cooking. Serve hot or cold.

SERVES 4 TO 6.

CHICKEN & BROCCOLI *stir fry*

1 clove garlic

1 small onion

1 head broccoli

1 red capsicum

500g boneless, skinless chicken

1 teaspoon grated root ginger

1 tablespoon soy sauce

2 tablespoons dry sherry

1 teaspoon sugar

2 teaspoons chicken stock powder

2 teaspoons cornflour

Crush, peel and chop garlic. Peel onion and cut into quarters, separating layers. Cut broccoli into florets. Peel broccoli stem and cut into strips. Cut capsicum in half and remove core. Cut flesh into thin strips. Cut chicken into thin strips. Spray or grease a wok or large frying pan with oil. Heat, then stir fry garlic, onion, ginger, broccoli and capsicum for 3 to 4 minutes. Remove from wok and set aside. Stir fry chicken for 2 to 3 minutes or until just cooked. Mix soy sauce, sherry, sugar, chicken stock powder and cornflour together. Return broccoli mixture to wok and pour in soy mixture. Heat through and serve immediately.

SERVES 4 TO 6.

STREET VENDOR
barbecued CHICKEN DRUMS

4 cloves garlic

1 teaspoon salt

2 teaspoons prepared chopped lemon grass

$1/4$ teaspoon chilli powder

1 teaspoon turmeric

1 teaspoon ground coriander

8 chicken drumsticks

Crush, peel and finely chop garlic. Mix garlic, salt, lemon grass, chilli powder, turmeric and coriander together in a plastic bag. Add chicken drumsticks and toss to coat. Refrigerate mixture overnight if possible or cook straightaway if necessary. Grill or barbecue chicken for 20 to 25 minutes or until juices run clear when tested.

SERVES 4.

lemon CHICKEN

LEMON SAUCE

1 tablespoon cornflour

$^1/_4$ cup lemon juice

1 tablespoon soy sauce

2 tablespoons sherry

1 teaspoon grated lemon rind

1 $^1/_2$ cups chicken stock

1 teaspoon grated root ginger

1 tablespoon brown sugar

CHICKEN

2 egg whites

$^1/_2$ cup cornflour

2 tablespoons water

350g chicken tenderloins

1 tablespoon oil

2 spring onions

LEMON SAUCE

In a saucepan mix cornflour, lemon juice, soy sauce and sherry together. Stir in remaining sauce ingredients. Bring to boil and cook, stirring, for 1 minute. Set aside.

CHICKEN

Lightly beat egg whites, cornflour and water together. Dip chicken in this. Heat oil in a pan and fry chicken until cooked. Trim spring onions. Cut diagonally into 1cm slices. Add to chicken. Pour Lemon Sauce over and serve.

SERVES 3 TO 4.

chilli TOMATO CHICKEN

3 single boneless, skinless
   chicken breasts
3 tablespoons cornflour
$1/2$ teaspoon salt
$1/4$ teaspoon five spice powder
$1/2$ cup chicken stock
2 tablespoons chilli sauce

$1/4$ cup tomato paste
2 cloves garlic
$1/4$ cup peanut oil
1 tablespoon finely chopped
   root ginger
Tomato slices
Snow pea sprouts

Cut chicken into thin strips. Mix cornflour, salt and five spice powder together in a plastic bag. Toss chicken in bag to coat with cornflour mixture. Mix chicken stock, chilli sauce and tomato paste together. Crush, peel and chop garlic. Heat two tablespoons of the oil in a wok or frying pan. Stir fry a quarter of the chicken at a time until brown and cooked. Remove from wok. Drain on absorbent paper and set aside while cooking remaining batches of chicken, adding more oil as necessary. Add garlic and ginger to wok and stir fry for 30 seconds. Add tomato paste mixture to wok. Bring to the boil. Return chicken to wok to heat through. Serve garnished with tomato slices and snow pea sprouts.

SERVES 4.

ginger CHICKEN

1 tablespoon cornflour
1 tablespoon soy sauce
500g chicken tenderloins
2 tablespoons grated root ginger
1 tablespoon white vinegar
1 teaspoon sugar
1 teaspoon ground ginger
$1/2$ teaspoon salt
100g snow peas
12 large spinach leaves
3 tablespoons peanut oil
Pickled ginger

Mix cornflour and soy sauce together and toss tenderloins in this. Set aside. Mix root ginger, vinegar, sugar, ground ginger and salt together. Trim snow peas and wash spinach. Heat oil in a wok or frying pan. Stir fry chicken for 2 to 3 minutes or until just cooked. Add ginger mixture, snow peas and spinach. Stir fry for 2 minutes. Serve immediately accompanied by pickled ginger.

SERVES 4.

apricot CHILLI CHICKEN WRAP

1 double boneless, skinless chicken breast
1 yellow capsicum
2 zucchini
6 dried apricots
1 cup chilli ginger sauce
3/4 cup couscous
1/2 teaspoon salt
1 1/4 cups boiling water
4 pieces baking paper 40 x 30cm

Cut chicken into 2cm slices. Cut capsicum in half, deseed and slice finely. Wash zucchini and slice finely. Chop apricots roughly and mix with chilli ginger sauce. Mix couscous and salt together in a bowl and pour boiling water over. Leave for 10 minutes. Divide couscous and chicken among baking paper sheets, placing mixture on one half of the paper. Cover with yellow capsicum and zucchini. Place apricot mixture on top. Fold over second half of paper and fold up edges of paper to seal. Place parcels on a baking tray and bake at 200°C for 20 minutes. Serve parcels snipped open.

SERVES 4.

spicy CHICKEN SAUCE

Serve over pasta of your choice.

250g boneless chicken meat such as tenderloins
1 onion
50g butter
$1/2$ teaspoon curry powder
$1/2$ teaspoon chilli powder
3 tablespoons flour
$1/2$ teaspoon salt
2 cups milk
1 tomato

Cut chicken into thin strips. Peel onion and chop finely. Melt butter in a saucepan and saute onion for 3 to 5 minutes or until soft but not coloured. Add curry powder and chilli powder and cook for 30 seconds to 1 minute or until spices smell fragrant. Stir in flour and salt and cook for 1 minute. Remove from heat and gradually stir in milk. Cook until sauce boils and thickens. Add chicken and cook for 3 to 5 minutes or until chicken is just cooked. Cut tomato in half. Remove seeds and cut flesh into small cubes. Serve over cooked, hot pasta.

MAKES ENOUGH SAUCE FOR 4 SERVINGS.

provencale CHICKEN SAUCE

Serve over pasta of your choice.

4 boneless, skinless chicken thighs
1 onion
2 cloves garlic
2 tablespoons oil
$1/2$ cup red wine
400g can tomatoes
2 tablespoons finely chopped parsley
$1/2$ cup black olives
Fresh basil leaves

Cut chicken into 1cm-wide strips. Peel onion and chop finely. Crush, peel and chop garlic. Heat oil in a saucepan and saute chicken, onion and garlic for 5 minutes. Add wine and bring to the boil. Drain tomatoes and cut into quarters, removing stem end. Add to wine mixture. Simmer for 5 minutes or until chicken is cooked. Mix parsley and olives together. Mix into sauce and pour over cooked, hot pasta. Garnish with basil leaves.

MAKES ENOUGH SAUCE FOR 4 SERVINGS.

CHICKEN & *prune* SAUCE

Serve over pasta of your choice.

1 onion
2 cloves garlic
1 tablespoon oil
1 cup pitted prunes
$1/2$ cup stuffed green olives
$1/4$ cup capers
1 cup dry white wine
200g chicken tenderloins
1 sprig rosemary

Peel onion and chop finely. Crush, peel and chop garlic. Heat oil in a saucepan and saute onion and garlic for 5 minutes or until clear. Add prunes, olives, capers and wine to saucepan. Bring to the boil and simmer for 5 minutes or until liquid is reduced by a quarter. Cut tenderloins in half lengthwise. Add to prune mixture and cook for 3 to 4 minutes or until chicken is cooked. Toss chicken mixture through cooked, hot pasta. Garnish with rosemary sprig.

MAKES ENOUGH SAUCE FOR 4 SERVINGS.

COCONUT CHICKEN *schnitzel*

WITH BANANA, YOGHURT & MINT SAUCE

1 egg
1 tablespoon water
1 tablespoon cornflour
4 chicken schnitzels
1 $^1/_2$ cups desiccated coconut

BANANA, YOGHURT
& MINT SAUCE
2 ripe bananas
$^1/_2$ cup unsweetened natural
   yoghurt
$^1/_4$ cup mango chutney
2 tablespoons chopped fresh
   mint

Lightly beat egg, water and cornflour together. Dip schnitzel into egg mixture. Coat with coconut. Place in an oiled roasting dish. Bake at 190°C for 10 minutes, turning halfway through cooking. Serve hot with Banana, Yoghurt & Mint Sauce.

BANANA, YOGHURT & MINT SAUCE

Peel bananas and mash until smooth. In a saucepan mix bananas, yoghurt, chutney and mint together. Heat until almost boiling and serve.

SERVES 4.

italian ROAST CHICKEN

WITH ARBORIO RICE

1 cup arborio rice
410g can tomato puree
2 cups chicken stock
1 medium chicken
2 tablespoons olive oil
2 tablespoons lemon juice
1 tablespoon dried rosemary
1 tablespoon dried sage
Fresh basil leaves

Place rice in a roasting dish. Pour tomato puree and chicken stock over rice. Bake at 180°C for 30 minutes. Remove giblets from chicken and tie legs together. Turn chicken wings under. Mix oil, lemon juice, rosemary and sage together. Rub over chicken. Place chicken on top of rice and cook for 1 hour or until juices run clear when tested. Serve chicken on rice garnished with torn basil leaves.

SERVES 4 TO 6.

fruity CHICKEN CASSEROLE

1 cup mixed dried fruit such as raisins, apricots and prunes

1 cup wine

1/4 cup honey

1 cup apple juice concentrate

1 chicken stock cube

1/2 teaspoon salt

1 onion

8 boneless, skinless chicken thighs

2 tablespoons cornflour

2 tablespoons water

1 tablespoon finely chopped parsley

Place dried fruit in a saucepan. Add wine, honey, apple juice, crumbled stock cube and salt. Bring to the boil. Remove from heat and leave to stand while preparing rest of ingredients. Peel and finely chop onion. Place chicken, onion and fruit mixture in a casserole dish. Cover and cook at 180°C for 50 to 55 minutes, or until cooked. Mix cornflour and water together. Mix into casserole. Cover and cook for a further 15 minutes. Garnish with chopped parsley.

SERVES 4 TO 6.

mediterranean

CHICKEN CASSEROLE

1 cup long-grain rice

8 skinless chicken pieces

1 onion

1 green capsicum

2 cloves garlic

425g can Italian tomatoes

440g can tomato puree

2 chicken stock cubes

$^1/_2$ cup pitted black olives

1 teaspoon oregano

1 $^1/_2$ cups water

2 teaspoons grated orange
   rind

$^1/_2$ teaspoon salt

Freshly ground black pepper

Sprinkle uncooked rice over base of a large casserole dish. Arrange chicken on top of rice. Peel and chop onion. Sprinkle over chicken. Deseed and chop capsicum. Sprinkle over onion. Crush, peel and chop garlic and sprinkle over chicken. Mix tomatoes, tomato puree, crumbled stock cubes, olives, oregano, water and orange rind together. Pour over chicken. Season to taste with salt and freshly ground black pepper. Cover and cook at 180°C for 1 $^1/_2$ hours, or until chicken and rice are cooked.

SERVES 4 TO 6.

apricot CHICKEN CASSEROLE

1 cup chopped dried apricots

1 cup water

8 skinless chicken pieces

35g packet onion soup mix

$^1/_2$ cup lemon juice

2 chicken stock cubes

1 cup hot water

1 tablespoon chopped parsley

Place apricots and first measure of water in a saucepan. Bring to the boil and simmer for 5 minutes while preparing rest of ingredients. Place chicken in a casserole dish. Mix soup mix, lemon juice, crumbled stock cubes and hot water together. Pour over chicken with apricots. Cover and cook at 180°C for 45 minutes or until chicken is cooked. Serve garnished with chopped parsley.

SERVES 4 TO 6.

COQ *au vin*

2 rashers bacon	2 tablespoons brandy
12 pickling onions	2 1/2 cups red wine
24 button mushrooms	2 cloves garlic
4 tablespoons oil	1 bouquet garni
1/2 cup flour	1 tablespoon flour
1/2 teaspoon salt	2 tablespoons water
Freshly ground black pepper	1 tablespoon finely chopped
6 whole chicken legs	parsley

Derind bacon and cut flesh into thin strips. Peel onions. Wipe and trim mushrooms. Heat one tablespoon of oil in a frying pan and cook bacon. Place in a casserole dish. Add onions and mushrooms to frying pan and saute for 5 minutes. Remove from pan and set aside. Mix flour, salt and pepper together in a plastic bag. Cut chicken legs at the joint. Toss chicken pieces in seasoned flour. Heat remaining oil in a large frying pan and brown chicken pieces on all sides. Warm brandy, pour over chicken and carefully ignite, using a long taper if possible. When flames subside, place chicken in a casserole dish. Add wine to brandy in pan. Stir to remove pan sediment. Pour over chicken. Crush, peel and mash garlic. Add bouquet garni and garlic to casserole. Cover and cook at 180°C for 45 minutes, stirring occasionally. Mix flour and water together and stir into chicken. Add mushrooms and onions and cook for a further 15 minutes. Remove bouquet garni and garlic and discard. Sprinkle casserole with chopped parsley.

SERVES 6.

QUICK CHICKEN & *cherry* CASSEROLE

If using the oven to cook this casserole, bake potatoes at the same time.

500g boneless, skinless chicken
680g jar pitted cherries
32g packet onion soup mix
2 tablespoons cider vinegar
$1/2$ cup chicken stock
1 tablespoon chopped parsley

Cut chicken into 2cm cubes. Place in a casserole dish or saucepan. Mix undrained cherries, soup mix, vinegar and chicken stock together. Pour over chicken. Cover and simmer on top of stove for 20 minutes, or bake at 180°C for 45 minutes. Serve garnished with parsley.

SERVES 4.

HANNAH'S DOUBLE CHICKEN *burgers*

Whenever I ask my kids what they fancy for dinner – and that makes a change from "What's for dinner, Mum?" – my daughter, Hannah, will always say "Chicken Burgers". How's that for inspiring? Here's my version. If you don't have hamburger buns on hand (I keep some in the freezer), use thick-cut slices of bread.

4 hamburger buns
8 frozen good quality chicken patties
$1/_2$ teaspoon Italian seasoning
Baby spinach leaves
Tomato slices
Readymade tahini sauce
1 tablespoon chopped parsley
Roughly chopped roasted peanuts

Cut buns into thirds horizontally. Toast cut sides if wished. Cook patties to packet directions, sprinkling with Italian seasoning halfway through cooking. Place a patty on bun bottom and middle. Top with spinach leaves, tomato slices, tahini sauce, parsley and peanuts. Assemble buns again and serve.

SERVES 4.

bengal PIZZA

Buy a pizza base for this recipe or use pita bread or make your own pizza base.

1 x 29cm pizza base
2 tablespoons green curry paste
1 tablespoon chilli oil
350g chicken tenderloins
$1/2$ cup fruit chutney
8 cucumber slices
$1/2$ cup unsweetened natural yoghurt
$1/4$ cup chopped fresh coriander

Spread pizza base with curry paste to within 1 cm from edge. Grill for about 2 minutes or until hot. Heat oil in a frying pan and cook tenderloins for 2 to 3 minutes or until cooked through. Top hot pizza base with chicken. Spoon chutney into middle of pizza with cucumber. Mix yoghurt and coriander together. Spoon over centre of pizza and serve immediately.

SERVES 2 TO 4.

CHICKEN *pie*

Use one cup of cold white sauce or unsweetened natural yoghurt instead of the sour cream in this dish if wished.

2 sheets flaky puff pastry	Salt
1 onion	Freshly ground black pepper
1 tablespoon oil	2 cups chopped cooked
1 tablespoon wholegrain	chicken
mustard	1 egg yolk
1 teaspoon dried tarragon	1 tablespoon water
250g pot low-fat sour cream	1 tablespoon sesame seeds

Place one sheet of pastry in a 13cm pie dish or cake tin. Peel onion and chop finely. Heat oil in a frying pan and saute onion for 5 minutes until clear. Mix onion, mustard, tarragon, sour cream, salt, pepper and chicken together. Fill pastry case in pie dish with this mixture. Wet edges of pastry. Place second sheet of pastry on top with points to the centre of each side of base pastry. Press edges together. Beat egg yolk and water together. Brush over surface of pastry, taking care not to brush over edges of pastry. Sprinkle with sesame seeds. Cut two steam holes in top of pie. Bake at 200°C for 15 to 20 minutes or until golden and cooked. Serve hot or cold.

SERVES 3 TO 4.

LEMON & *ginger* CHICKEN

LEMON & GINGER SAUCE

1 tablespoon cornflour

1/4 cup lemon juice

1 tablespoons soy sauce

2 tablespoons sherry

1 teaspoon grated lemon rind

1 1/2 cups chicken stock

1 teaspoon grated root ginger

1 tablespoon brown sugar

CHICKEN

2 egg whites

1/2 cup cornflour

2 tablespoons water

350g chicken tenderloins

1 tablespoon oil

2 spring onions

LEMON & GINGER SAUCE

Mix cornflour with lemon juice, soy sauce and sherry. Mix lemon rind, stock, ginger, brown sugar and cornflour mixture together in a saucepan. Bring to the boil and cook for 1 minute. Set side while preparing chicken.

CHICKEN

Lightly beat egg whites, cornflour and water together. Dip chicken in this mixture. Heat oil in a wok or frying pan and stir fry chicken until juices run clear when tested. Trim spring onions and cut into 1cm slices on the diagonal. Add to chicken, pour Lemon Sauce over and serve.

SERVES 3 TO 4.

QUICK *roast* CHICKEN

Roasts are always popular. Here's a quick version for those with limited time but a hankering for comfort food.

4 chicken legs
¼ cup Italian seasoned oil
1 tablespoon lemon pepper seasoning
1 teaspoon Mexican chilli powder
6 potatoes
24 cloves garlic
Torn basil leaves to garnish

Place chicken in a large roasting dish. Brush with oil. Pour remaining oil into roasting dish. Mix lemon pepper seasoning and chilli powder together. Sprinkle over chicken. Peel potatoes and cut into 2cm cubes. Add to roasting dish. Toss to coat in oil. Add garlic cloves. Bake at 190°C for 40 to 45 minutes or until chicken is cooked and potatoes are golden. Serve on a platter garnished with torn basil leaves.

SERVES 4.

index